Reinaldo Domingos

Money Boy
Little Citizen

1st Edition

About the series

The series "Money Boy" is a children's adaptation based upon the DSOP Financial Education Methodology, conceived by master, professor, educator, and financial therapist Reinaldo Domingos.

The series is part of the DSOP Financial Education Program that ranges from grammar school to college. It consists of 30 didactic volumes (15 textbooks and 15 teacher's books) and six paradidactic volumes that comprise subjects of family, diversity, sustainability, autonomy, and citizenship.

In addition to the books, the schools that adopt the DSOP Financial Education Program are entitled to pedagogical training, financial education workshops for teachers, lectures for the students and the community, and access to the school website (portalescolas.dsop.com.br), which consists of class plans, interactive activities (games), videos, and exclusive access to students, teachers, parents, and school managers.

For further information, please visit www.dsop.com.br/escolas or contact a local franchisee in your area by searching on our website www.dsop.com.br/franquia.

What's happening

In Lagoa Branca town, Money Boy, Spender, Victoria and Caroline venture in dreams that require them to be independent and grow up.

By going through the rite of passage from childhood to pre-adolescence, the daily lives of the characters undergo changes: they learn how to manage their allowances, practice the **DSOP Methodology** to fulfill dreams, become entitled to the right to come and go in town by themselves and experience their first love.

Spender falls in love but it is not corresponded. Victoria and Caroline try to convince their parents that they can go through the city by themselves. And Money Boy comes up with a plan to save money to take a trip to the city where his grandparents live.

Will they be able them to achieve the autonomy they are looking for? This is yet another one episode of the challenging and catching series that became popular among children and teenagers in hundreds of schools in Brazil! Are you curious? Embark on this plot and have a nice journey you too.

© Editora DSOP, 2016
© Reinaldo Domingos, 2015

President
Reinaldo Domingos

Text editor
Andrei Sant'Anna
Renata de Sá

Art editor
Denise Patti Vitiello
Christine Baptista

Illustrator
Ariel Fajtlowicz

Editorial producer
Amanda Torres

Translator
Joan Rumph
Milena Cavichiolo

All rights reserved to Editora DSOP
Av. Paulista, 726 - Cj. 1210 - Bela Vista
ZIP Code: 01310-910 - Brazil - São Paulo - SP
Phone: 11 3177-7800
www.editoradsop.com.br

Dados Internacionais de Catalogação na Publicação (CIP)
(Câmara Brasileira do Livro, SP, Brasil)

```
Domingos, Reinaldo
    Money boy : little citizen / Reinaldo Domingos ;
illustration Ariel Fajtlowicz ; translation Joan
Rumph e Milena Cavichiolo. -- São Paulo : Editora
DSOP, 2015.

    Título original: O menino do dinheiro : pequeno
cidadão
    ISBN 978-85-8276-107-6


    1. Dinheiro - Literatura infantojuvenil
2. Finanças - Literatura infantojuvenil
I. Fajtlowicz, Ariel. II. Título.


14-11827                                        CDD-028.5
```

Índices para catálogo sistemático:

1. Educação financeira : Literatura infantil
   028.5
2. Educação financeira : Literatura infantojuvenil
   028.5

Contents

A great party 7

The mysterious letter 11

The tune den 15

Achieving independence 19

Dear grandpa 27

Financial independence 33

A few extra bucks 41

So near, so faraway 45

The month of June 51

Flowers to you! 55

Ready to takeoff 61

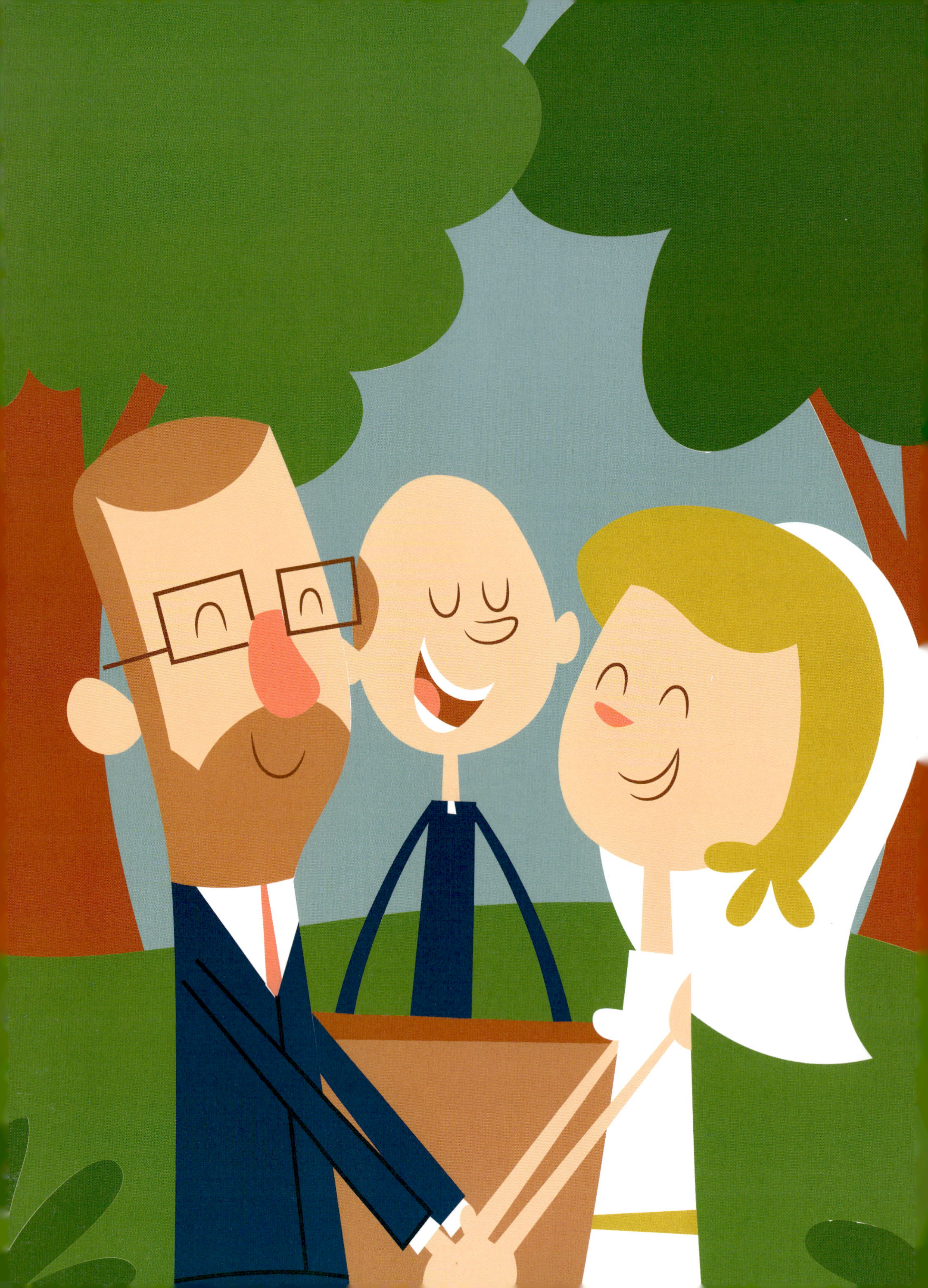

A great party

January welcomed the New Year in the city of Lagoa Branca. The local people looked forward to this special day, for it meant there would be a great party that night.

The preparations were at full speed at Daisy´s Square. Teenagers and children alike decorated the open area with colorful flags and ribbons tied to the tree branches.

Money Boy and Victoria helped a group of people decorate the largest tree in the square—a green, leafy oak tree. They placed blinking lights around the tree, which brought out the natural beauty of the environment.

In the middle of the buzz around the square, Money Boy's cell phone rang with a text from his friend Caroline:

"I'm on my way with my mom. I'll be there soon to help you and to enjoy the party! Please tell Victoria. See you, Caroline."

Money Boy texted her back, "Hi, Caroline! We're happy you're coming back! It is crazy here. Come soon. We are waiting for you. See you, MB."

Caroline had been away on her uncle's small farm and only talked to her friends by e-mail or text message. She missed them greatly and wanted to see them as soon as possible. It would be a very special occasion by the way, because many people would be attending the event.

The upcoming wedding of Mr. Custodio, Spender's father, and Ms. Help, Spender's teacher, generated much happiness and the presence of so many local people. Mr. Custodio and Ms. Help had been dating for a year and decided to get married.

Despite the Custodio family being very wealthy, Ms. Help, a humble woman who liked nature, didn't want a fussy party and chose Daisy's Square as the scenery to such an important day in her life.

Spender, happy and excited, had been dreaming about having a little brother and now that possibility seemed a lot closer.

In just a few hours before the ceremony, Daisy's Square had transformed into a wonderland of lights and flowers. The guests talked cheerfully as they waited for the bride to arrive.

Spender seemed nervous and Victoria tried to calm him down, but he could not focus on the words of his friend. At that moment, Caroline arrived with her mother and went up to meet her friends.

The blonde-haired girl noticed the look of concern on Spender's face. She gave him a long hug and stood next to him holding his hand.

Spender quickly felt at ease and a few minutes later, the bride came walking down a carpet of white flowers covering the ground.

Ms. Help smiled as she held a flower bouquet and looked tenderly at her husband-to-be, Mr. Custodio. She had the same tenderness in her eyes when she glanced at Spender.

The couple said "yes" under the open skies before family and friends, and at that time even the daisies in the square were surrounded with joy. Right after that, a band started to play and everyone moved to the dance floor.

Caroline, who was very fond of writing and imagining things, took her block of notes and wrote down things she heard and saw. In her mind, the party looked like the final chapter of a book.

However, the story of the New Year in the town of Lagoa Branca had just begun. Within a few days, the kids would resume their studies and the challenges they would have to face would be even greater than last year's.

But Money Boy and his friends did not fear new things. Always ready for an adventure, they believed the greater the challenge, the bigger the reward that comes with it!

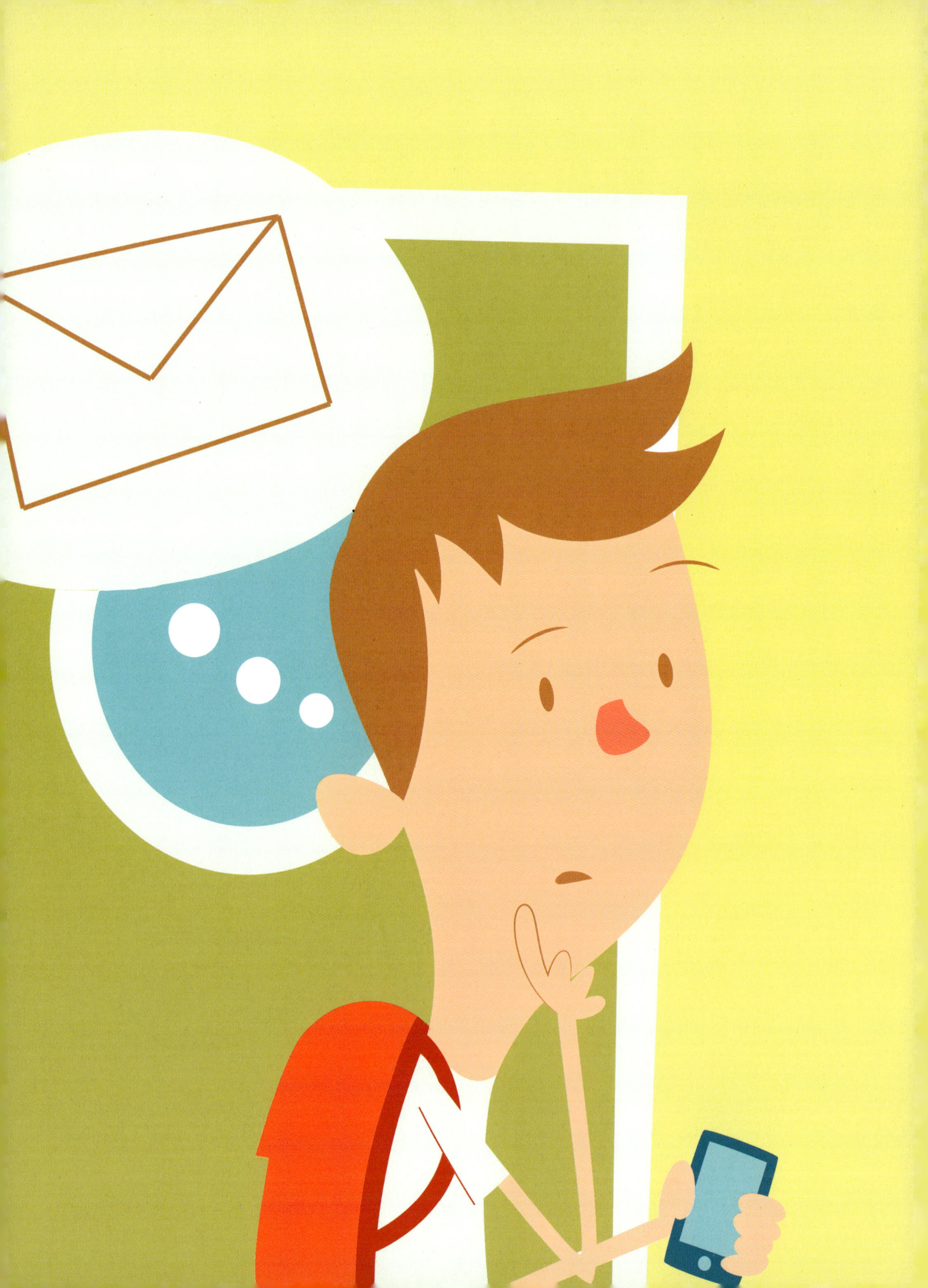

The mysterious letter

One week after the great party that rocked the town of Lagoa Branca, the students gathered back at the schoolyard on a beautiful, sunny day.

Money Boy was on his way to school when he heard his cell phone ringing. He took the phone expecting to find a text from his friend Spender saying he would be late once again.

But to his surprise, Mrs. Foresight, his mother, left a message.

"Son, I'm out shopping and will be back late! Your sister will stay at your aunt's until I come back. I left your lunch in the fridge. When you come back home just heat it up. Ah, I almost forgot, there is a letter for you. It is on top of your bedside table. Love, Mom."

The boy felt restless. What kind of letter could that be? Who still writes letters nowadays instead of sending an email? Why didn't his mother mention the sender's name?

Even with his mind overflowing with questions, the boy put away his phone and walked swiftly to school. He turned it off though, because he knew the school did not allow the use of cell phones during class time.

He entered the classroom and sat in the same seat he had always taken. Thirty minutes later, Spender easily slipped into the room, hoping no one would notice. The students, of course, did not let it go and the room erupted into silly noises. Some students whistled, others clapped their hands and made jokes of the boy known for being tardy.

Spender took a seat next to his friends while the teacher quieted the students in order to continue with the lesson.

Victoria, looking at the trees through the window, thought about the conversation with her father during breakfast. He mentioned a dream from his youth that he never achieved. Mr. Carrera wanted to play drums in the school band, but time passed and his dream faded. Soon, he forgot all about it.

Victoria had some musical talent. Throughout her childhood, she had a good ear for music and could recognize the sounds of different instruments as well as identify the chords in a song. She would roughly play a few tunes on a small keyboard she had received for her seventh birthday.

Victoria always thought it would be great to learn how to play the guitar, but she put off doing anything about it. However, her dream had come alive again after the conversation with her father, and she felt inspired to find a music school to develop her skill.

Only one good music school existed in Lagoa Branca, and it was located on the other side of town. It would take a bus ride and a long walk to arrive at The Tune Den.

Victoria searched the map on her computer for directions and found the school in a neighborhood called Harmony.

Caroline sat beside the girl with dimples and asked why she needed a map. Victoria revealed her plan to take guitar lessons at The Tune Den.

The two of them talked and Caroline felt encouraged to learn how to play an instrument as well. The hardest part would be convincing their moms to let them take a bus and go by themselves to the northern part of town.

At that point, they were so lost in their conversation they didn't realize the teacher had given the class a new assignment. Caroline, completely taken by Victoria's idea, began dreaming about the music school.

That reminded her of an old tale her grandmother used to tell her called "A flute's dream." Since then, she had nurtured the wish of one day learning how to play that instrument. Now her friend Victoria had teased her by mentioning The Tune Den. Caroline thought that perhaps the time had come.

The students did not show very much interest in the first class after vacation. It would take a little time before they would get used to the school routine of homework, assignments, and exams once again.

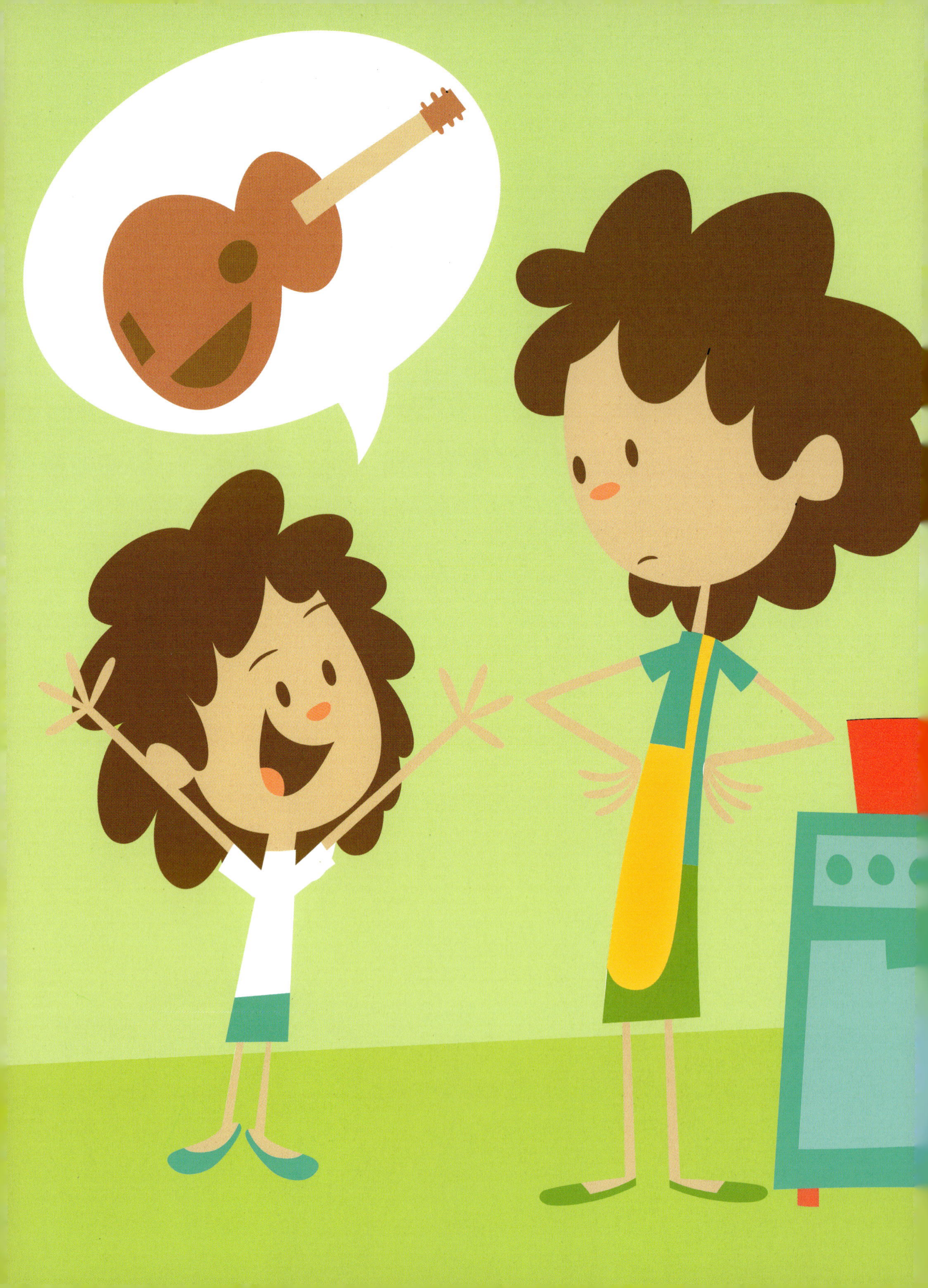

The tune den

Victoria came home and saw her mother who was cooking lunch. She thought that was an appropriate moment to talk about her wish to begin guitar classes at The Tune Den.

Mrs. Efficiency listened very carefully to her daughter, but two things concerned her: the cost of the guitar lessons and the long distance from home to the music school.

"But mom, I have already searched the internet. I can take the bus from Daisy's Square to Harmony and I will be there in about half an hour," the girl pleaded.

"I know that, dear. However, you have never been that far by yourself in a bus. I would be very worried each time you left, and I cannot manage dropping you off and picking you up because of my job," said Mrs. Efficiency. "But I will not be going alone," Victoria persisted. "Caroline is planning to take flute classes there, too. We could go together."

"Does her mother know about that?"

"Not yet. They will talk about it today."

"Then let us wait and see how it goes. Meanwhile, I will talk to your dad and see what he thinks, okay?" Mrs. Efficiency assured her daughter.

Victoria walked over to the kitchen sink and began to help her mother with the food preparation. The girl imagined her father arriving home soon and supporting her plan to take music lessons.

When Money Boy dashed through the door at his house, he raced up the stairs to his room, anxious to read the mysterious letter. The envelope was addressed "From Raymond" and "To Raymond."

He thought that was so weird and did not exactly get what it meant. After the initial surprise, he opened the envelope and read the letter.

> Dear Ray,
>
> How are you doing, young man?
> I miss you very much, so I decided to write you this letter. I got my new glasses this week, which makes it easier to write. Here in Recife, Brazil, it is very hot, but when the wind blows, the temperature becomes quite pleasant.
> Recently, I was wondering when will you be coming to visit me? I want to show you around town. There are many wonderful things to see. Come have some coconut water with me while we take a stroll by the boardwalk. I want to take you to the town market and the art market, too.
> Life is good and time flies by so quickly. Please come soon!
>
> Love,
> Grandpa Raymond

Money Boy folded the letter and kept it in a drawer at his bedside table. His grandpa was kind and it had been a long time since he last spoke to him. He had so many things to tell him.

The boy had already asked his parents to take him to the city where his grandpa lived, but they could not afford the expensive trip. Airfare tickets, depending on the season, can be very expensive, and the boy was too young to travel by himself on such a journey.

However, he would turn 13 years old this year and would start planning that dream. The letter from his grandpa was an invitation to an adventure, and Ray didn't want to miss that opportunity.

Meanwhile, an intense conversation continued between Caroline and her mother. The girl tried to convince her mother that at 12 years old, she was old enough to go across town by bus to take flute lessons at the music school.

"But dear, you do not know the way. You have never even taken a bus before. You might get lost. Streets can be dangerous," the mother said, trying to reason with her daughter.

Finally, Caroline suggested something that convinced her mother at last.

"Then I have a solution for that. Money Boy can come with us. Victoria and I will meet him at Daisy's Square to take the bus to Harmony together," Caroline announced.

"Well, Money Boy is a little older than you and he sure is a sensible kid. If his parents and Victoria's parents agree to it, I don't see a problem," the mother said, giving in to her daughter's wish.

Caroline ran around the house celebrating her achievement. She had to text Victoria to tell her about it. Next, she needed to convince Money Boy to be their chaperone, so he could keep company with the girls as they traveled to The Tune Den.

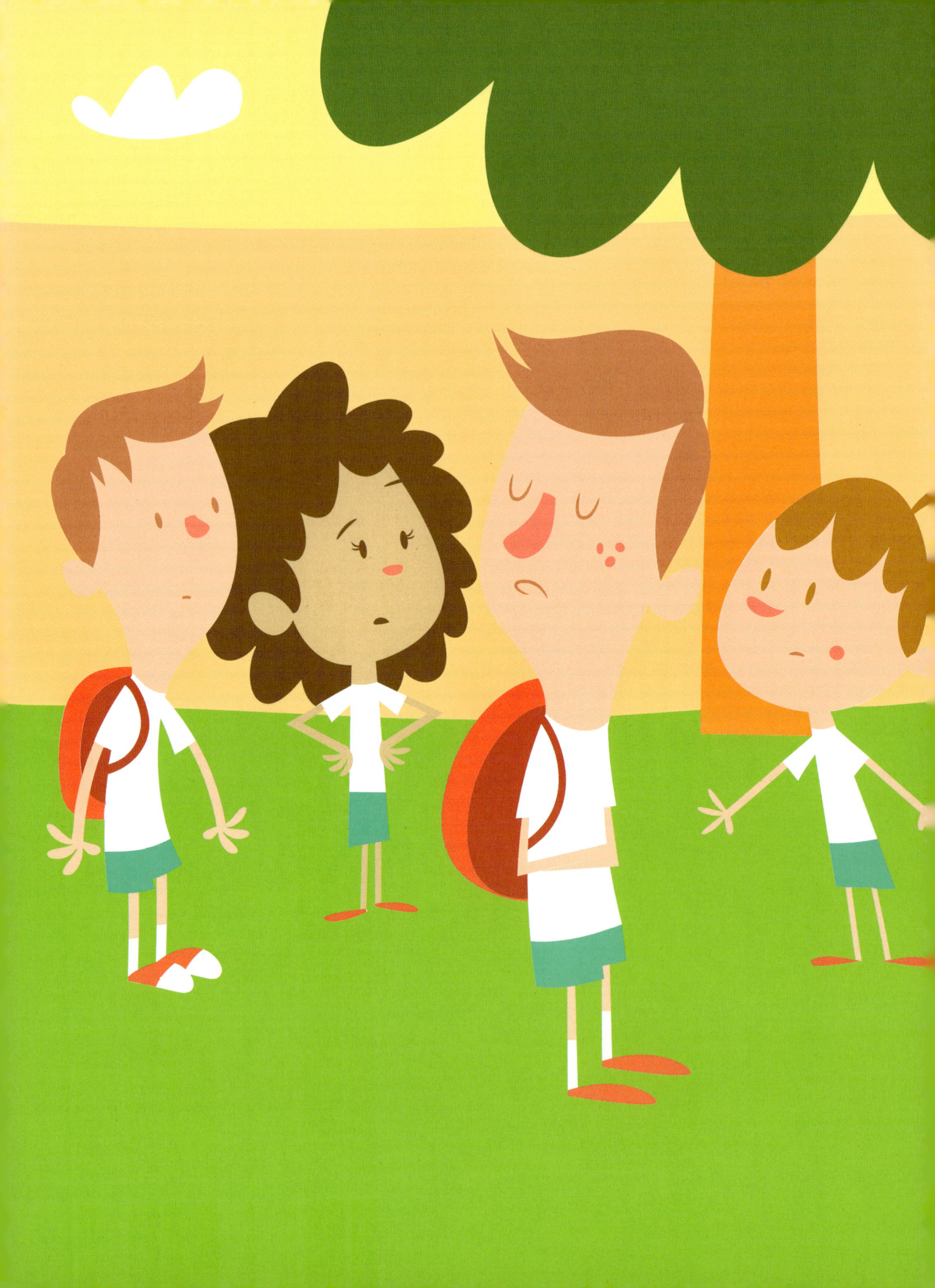

Achieving independence

The next day, Caroline and Victoria anxiously waited for Money Boy to arrive at the schoolyard. He would play an important role in their plans to enroll at The Tune Den music school.

"Money Boy is late today!" Caroline observed. "Maybe he isn't coming at all."

"I don't know. But if he skips school today, we can drop by his place after class," Victoria said.

"Tell me something, why didn't your mothers choose me to be the guy to take you to Harmony?" asked Spender. "Does it have to be only Money Boy? Like nobody else knows the way!"

"What's up Spender boy? Are you jealous?" Caroline asked sarcastically.

"Our mothers won't trust a guy like you!" Victoria said, laughing.

"What's so funny?" demanded Spender.

Ten minutes later, Money Boy appeared at the school gate bearing his backpack. The boy approached his friends and said he wanted to tell them something.

"What news is that? Please don't tell us it's another little sister!" said Spender, still in a mood that made his friends laugh at him.

"No way," said Money Boy.

"Ah, I don't know. Last time you came here to tell us something new, your mother was pregnant!" Spender said.

"No! It's nothing like that. Yesterday, I got a letter from my grandpa in Brazil," said Money Boy. "He invited me to visit the town where he lives and I started to think seriously about it. I want to make the trip, but I don't know yet how to plan for it. It's a huge dream of mine."

"Well, we can help you, if you help us!" said Victoria with a grin.

"What's up with you, Victoria? What are you up to now?" Money Boy asked.

The girls explained their plan. Spender stood to the side, still feeling annoyed that the girls had not considered him to escort them to Harmony.

"Well, I understand your request, but there's still one thing missing from your scheme," said Money Boy.

"And what is that?" Caroline asked.

"If I take you, then I'll have to wait around for an hour and a half until the end of your class. I don't know anybody who lives there or anything about the Harmony area. How am I going to spend the time waiting for you two princesses before you are ready to go back home?" asked Money Boy with a smile on his face.

"Well, we hadn't thought about that," Victoria acknowledged.

"That's it! I don't want to hang out alone for an hour and a half, unless..." Money Boy uttered, pausing to get their attention.

"Unless?" the two girls repeated

"Well, unless Spender comes with us. That way we can hang out together," said Money Boy.

Victoria and Caroline looked at each other surprised. Their dream of playing a musical instrument all came down to Spender. If he refused to come along now, it would be a lot more complicated to convince Money Boy to follow their plan.

"Now you two will have to apologize to me!" Spender said, laughing.

"How's that? What are you talking about?" asked Money Boy.

"Before you arrived these two ladies were picking on me. They even said their mothers would never trust a guy like me," Spender replied.

"Girls, did you really say that? Shame on you! I think you should apologize to Spender," said Money Boy. "We know he's kind of a complainer, but he's a good friend who can be counted on."

Victoria and Caroline didn't' have a choice but to apologize to their friend. The boy, satisfied with their gesture, agreed to escort the girls to The Tune Den during the first weeks of class.

The four were smiling happily when Mr. Raymoney came by and asked, "What's new?" The girls told him about their desire to learn how to play a musical instrument and the difficulty of convincing their parents to let them go across town on a bus to attend classes at Harmony.

Money Boy talked about the trip he intended to take to visit his grandpa. He knew he would have a hard time convincing his parents to let him take the plane alone, and he would have to come up with the money to pay for the airline ticket.

Mr. Raymoney took this opportunity to start asking many questions. "Have you already searched and compared prices for that trip? How is your financial health these days? Isn't it time to diagnose and redirect your budget? As far as I'm concerned, your trip is a long-term dream. Don't you think?" the teacher asked, addressing the four friends.

"It's true! I think you could apply the **DSOP Methodology** and start saving money to take that trip at the end of the year," Victoria agreed.

"As for your parents, I think your grandfather could talk to them and ask to let you go, since you're turning thirteen," added Caroline.

"That's right! You're reaching an age in which the search for independence begins and it is necessary!" Mr. Raymoney said.

"What do you mean, teacher? What's independence?" Spender asked.

"Well, independence is having the freedom to do things. You're striving for your own right to come and go. You want to go out without being watched by your parents, and you wish to experience things without depending on anyone. The girls want to take a bus to town without having an adult nearby. Money Boy wants to take a plane to a city far away. You are searching for independence," Mr. Raymoney explained

"Gee, what about me?" asked Spender. "I think I don't want anything close to that at the moment."

"Don't be sad and don't be worried. At the right time, the wish for more independence will also come upon you," the teacher said.

Mr. Raymoney wished everyone good luck and walked away. The bell rang and he had another class to teach.

Victoria and Caroline took their backpacks and walked to class. Spender and Money Boy followed behind them, still talking about dreams and independence. The topic of having more independence would dominate their conversations from now on.

Over the next week, Victoria and Caroline anxiously counted the days remaining before their first lesson at The Tune Den. Their parents had already agreed to their enrollment at the music school, especially since Money Boy and Spender would be accompanying them. The girls would have lunch at their homes and meet up at Daisy's Square to take the bus to Harmony.

The day came and at 3 PM, Money Boy and Spender waited for the girls at the bus stop. Caroline's father, who was divorced from her mother and lived in another town, had agreed to pay for the lessons. Mr. Carrera raised Victoria's allowance. He told his daughter that she should manage her money by taking the responsibility of paying for her music lessons.

When the bus arrived, the four friends hopped on, carrying their backpacks with a feeling of freedom and anticipation.

They were like adventurers marching into town. They rarely traveled to areas far from their homes and now, looking out the window, they were exploring new sites. They were learning the street names, catching a glance at the old theater building and the red brick church. They also spotted Big Mouth, a snack bar well known for its delicious cheese sandwiches.

When the girls arrived at The Tune Den, Money Boy and Spender decided they would explore the neighborhood.

"You know, I am kind of worried because I don't have a dream of my own to go after," said Spender. "Am I really that boring?"

"Stay cool! That comes with time," advised Money Boy. "When you least expect it, something you really want will come up. Give it some time."

"Yeah, you're right. It's just that I'm kind of down lately."

"Tell me, how are your plans for the trip?" asked Spender. "Have you looked at the ticket fares yet? Have you talked to your parents?"

"Yes, I've searched for tickets. If I buy them well ahead of the departure date, I can get them cheaper. But to sum it up, I have to save $1,500 at least to travel in November or December," Money Boy said.

"Gee, that much? How do you intend to come up with that much money?" Spender asked.

"Well, I'll save all that I can. Besides, I'm asking my closest relatives to give me money as a birthday present this year. This way I'll be saving. I made a new diagnosis, I know what I earn each month, and I'll stick to a tight budget and avoid any extra expenses," Money Boy explained.

"But at the end of the year the air tickets are very expensive. I've heard my dad talking about it. Why don't you travel at the beginning of July when we are on vacation?" Spender suggested.

"I don't think I can save that much money in such a short time. It would be six months from now," replied Money Boy.

"Well, if the airline tickets are half the price, then maybe you could make it. Have you checked that already? How much would the tickets be in July?" asked Spender.

"Well I haven't done it yet. I don't know," answered Money Boy.

"Hold on! I have an idea. I have my notebook in my backpack. Let's do some internet searching."

"Good one. Let's go!"

The two of them went over to the ice cream store and sat down to search several airline websites.

"Check this one here," said Spender. "If you travel at night and come back early in the morning, it's not that expensive. Summing it all up, you can buy a ticket for $650."

"Wow, it is very cheap. How can that be?" asked Money Boy.

"Well, I think it must be off-season. Besides, when everybody wants to travel at the same time, the prices skyrocket. My father always complains about that," Spender said.

"Look, I think I can save $650 by the end of the semester," Money Boy said.

"Yes! And if you don't manage to save all that money, maybe your parents could help you," advised his friend.

"Ah, but I don't want them to have any extra expenses. I want to do it all by myself."

"Look, I always ask my father for help when I want to buy something," confessed Spender.

"Remember that independence thing the teacher was talking to us about the other day? If we are always relying on our parents, we will never become independent, and we will never grow up," argued the boy.

"It's true! I don't want to be treated like a child anymore. I have grown up, and my father and my stepmother keep treating me like a little baby," Spender said.

"Well, perhaps you'll have to find a way to show them that you've grown up and are becoming independent," Money Boy suggested.

"Maybe that's right," admitted Spender. "I'll give it some thought."

"Yes, do it! You're not that boring, Spender. And, you've just given me an idea that will help me in my trip planning. Actually, it is wiser to travel in July rather than in December. You're a genius, man!" Money Boy said, joking with his friend.

At that moment, the waiter approached them bringing two huge ice cream cups on a tray. Money Boy and Spender enjoyed them and kept talking.

At The Tune Den, Caroline and Victoria were taken to separate classrooms. After all, they wanted to learn different instruments. They filled out their applications and took a test so the instructors could evaluate their music skill levels.

Victoria played a song on the guitar and impressed the teacher, who told her she was truly gifted.

For Caroline, the flute proved to be a tougher instrument to play. However, the instructor advised her to be patient and not to give up, because she had gone there to learn. If she already knew how to play, there would be no reason to take lessons. The girl then smiled and looked a little more confident.

On their way out, the girls met Money Boy and Spender, who were waiting for them at the front door. There was a lot to talk about on their way back home.

The four friends took their seats on the bus heading back to Daisy's Square. The girls continued to talk about the tests they took, the instructors, and the other students they met. They realized they had a new problem to solve: the purchase of a guitar and a flute.

Without instruments, Victoria and Carolina could not practice at home. They could only practice with the flute and the guitar they borrowed at The Tune Den during classes.

The girls did not want to ask their parents for help anymore, since they were already paying for the music school tuition.

Money Boy worried about his financial situation, too. He now had a long-term dream, to take a trip to visit his grandfather.

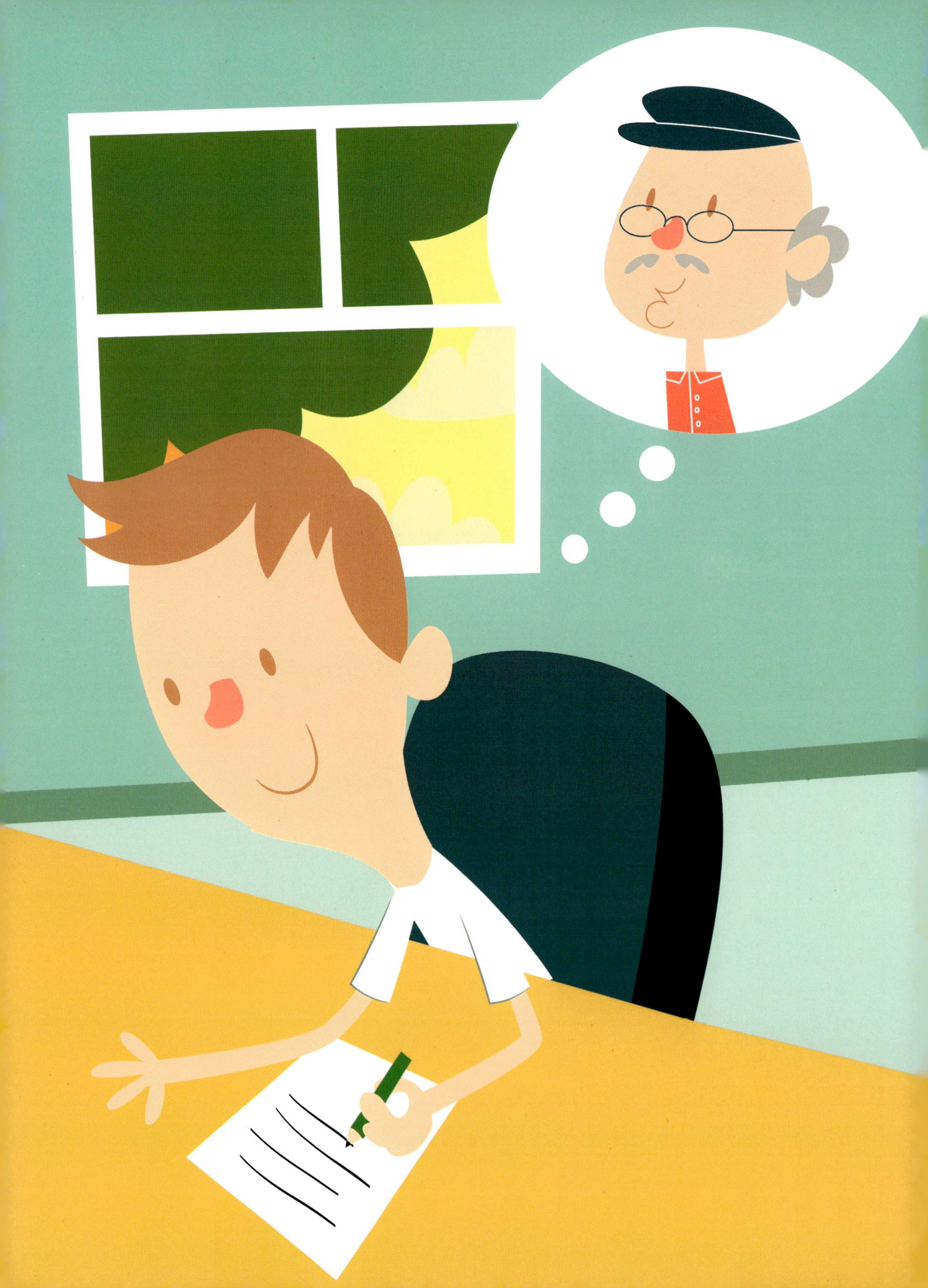

Dear grandpa

Another sunny day began in the little town of Lagoa Branca. Victoria stretched up in bed while she recalled the details of a very happy dream. She dreamed she had received a guitar from her fairy godmother.

After breakfast, Victoria called Caroline and told her all about it.

"Victoria, you know that's too childish! Fairy godmothers don't exist," Caroline said on the phone, smiling.

"I know that, I know that!" repeated Victoria. "It was just a good dream and I was so happy!"

"Then it's about time we come up with a plan to make that dream come true in real life. By the way, let's make it our dream, because I want to buy my flute, too," Caroline continued.

"All right, but I don't see how we can do it. Our parents are already paying for our music lessons and our money isn't worth that much. Mr. Raymoney once told me children aren't allowed to work. My father won't agree to that either," Victoria responded.

"Well, while you were talking, I thought to myself, is it true our money isn't worth that much? For real?" asked Caroline. "Last year, when you taught me the **DSOP Methodology**, I found out that I was wasting my money on a lot of foolish things. When I made that diagnosis, I could see that. Afterwards, I started spending less and even managed to purchase my tablet!"

"Yes, good idea! We can do a diagnosis and reorganize our expenses. We can take better care of our money, but even if we do, I don't think we'll be able to purchase our instruments that soon," Victoria said.

"Let's think a little more about that. There must be a faster way to get that money," Caroline suggested.

"Well, if you know one, please tell me!" said Victoria. "I'll have to hang up now because my mother is calling. See you!"

At Money Boy's house, the sun shined through the windows and woke up everyone. The sun wasn't the only thing to awaken the family. Little Gabriela's crying had also caused Mrs. Foresight and Mr. Unaware to jump out of bed earlier than usual.

Money Boy heard his little sister crying and picked her up into his arms. While his mother prepared warm milk, the boy sang her a lullaby as he walked around the living room.

After feeding, the baby once again calmed down and fell asleep. Mrs. Foresight started to do the laundry, and Money Boy locked himself in his room to answer his grandpa's letter.

Dear Grandpa,

Your letter cheered me up. I want to visit your town and give you a big hug! We all miss you and granny.

This year, I'll be turning 13. I think it's a great age to think big. I mean, I've always thought big, but now I can think even bigger!

I've never taken a trip alone and want so much to do it to meet you.

But there are two things in my way. The first one is that I must convince to my parents to let me take the plane by myself. I'd really like them to come with me, but my little sister Gaby is too small, and we would also need airline tickets for everybody. It would be too expensive.

The second thing that makes my trip difficult is the money to pay for the airline tickets. I am already taking care of that. I've been practicing the four steps of the DSOP Methodology to save enough money to make my dream come true and come to visit you in your town.

That's it for now. Please wait, it might take a while. You said life goes fast, but we need some extra time for our big dreams!

A hug from your grandson,
Money Boy

As soon as he finished writing, Money Boy walked to the post office to send his grandfather the letter. Then he went over to school, as it was about time for the first class to begin.

There he met Victoria and Spender who were heading to the class where Mr. Raymoney was waiting for the students. Written on the board, the class subject was easily noticeable: Independence.

When everybody had taken their seats, Mr. Raymoney began the class by welcoming them and posing a challenging question:

"Does anyone here know what independence is?" he asked.

Everyone remained silent. Some of them thought they knew it, but nobody dared to raise their hands to give an exact answer.

"Well, since nobody wants to take a chance, I'll ask another question. Which words come to your mind when you hear someone speaking about independence?" the teacher said.

"Autonomy!" shouted Money Boy.

"Freedom," said Manuela in the back of the class.

"Liberty to come and go," remarked Victoria.

"To be able to travel alone," Spender said.

"To be able to buy things we want without having to ask our parents," said Caroline.

"Very good! Independence is a mix of several of the things you've mentioned. Now I want to know, who in the class wants to be independent?" Mr. Raymoney asked.

All the students raised their hands supporting their desire for independence and the teacher smiled.

"And why do you want that? What do you intend to do when you get more independence?" the teacher asked.

"Well, I intend to take a trip alone," answered Money Boy.

"I want my mother to trust me and allow me to take a bus to go to places by myself, even if they are far from where I live," argued Caroline.

"I want to learn how to drive, but my parents keep saying I still don't have independence for that!" complained Philip.

"I want to earn my own money. I want to be independent to work and buy a guitar," Victoria stated.

"Well, from what I hear, having independence is part of everyone's dream in this classroom," concluded Mr. Raymoney.

The students nodded and the teacher continued.

"It's important that everyone understands there are different kinds of independence. Each type will come at the right time for each one here. I'll write them on the board and what you must do to achieve them," said the teacher.

All the students stared at the board. Mr. Raymoney listed the different kinds of independence.

Independence is a word of Greek origin whose meaning is related to autonomy, freedom, or self-sufficiency.

Individual Independence is the one that assures our right to come and go. When we have more independence, we can move around town and even take a trip, within the country or even abroad. To have individual independence, we must first prove that we are responsible enough to manage that freedom. In addition, we need to know where we are heading and understand the sort of problems that might come up during our journey. It's always good to bear in mind that our parents won't be available. We will have to solve any problems that happen by ourselves.

Citizen Independence is a set of rights that all citizens must behold, as granted by the government of the country they live in. Some of those rights are public health (good public hospitals for the general public), education (good public schools for children), household (government initiatives that make that possible), sanitation, elections (granting of rights for anyone to vote after they become a certain age), etc. That independence is a right granted to every citizen.

The class was almost over when Mr. Raymoney told the students they would study the third kind of independence in their next class. To speed up things, the teacher revealed that he would talk about Financial Independence, and they needed to pay careful attention.

THE TUNE DEN

Financial independence

Several days later, Caroline and Victoria traveled to The Tune Den escorted by their two friends.

Despite the kindness of Money Boy and Spender, what the girls really wanted was to have their parents' permission to go into town by themselves. However, while that permission had not been granted, Money Boy and Spender were doing their best to take them to Harmony.

As they were leaving the music school, absent-minded Spender walked down the street while his friend stepped away to make a call on his cellphone. Suddenly, Spender bumped into a long, curly-haired girl who was walking in the opposite direction and carrying a saxophone.

The papers she carried fell down on the ground and Spender apologized for being so distracted as he help her pick them up.

He noticed they were not ordinary papers but musical scores. He also noticed the girl was very pretty and had a soft, sweet voice. His heart began pumping faster.

"My name is Laura! And yours?" she asked.

"My name is Spender."

"Do you study at The Den too?"

"Yes!" Spender mumbled, without knowing what he was saying.

"Oh, that's cool! Which instrument do you play?"

"Well, I'm still learning, but I play drums. Yes, drums it is... my instrument," he stuttered.

"Wow, that's awesome!" said Laura. "Well, I have to go! See you around next Thursday, right?"

The boy nodded and the girl walked the opposite way. Still stunned by her kindness and beauty, he didn't notice Money Boy had come closer and began speaking to him.

"What happened, Spender?" Money Boy asked. "Your face is as white as a sheet."

"Man, you're not going to believe what just happened," answered Spender, still dizzy.

The boy's heart calmed down and he spoke about Laura to Money Boy. Soon afterwards, Victoria and Caroline came out of the music school and all four of them took the bus back to their place.

Spender, casually, asked his friends how he could enroll at the music school and said he wished to become a drum player.

Both the girls laughed and didn't even realize, behind that interest in joining the music school, there was a girl called Laura.

The next day, the class was in a great mood because they would learn about financial independence in Mr. Raymoney's class. The idea of financial independence was on the minds of all the students.

Money Boy had a long-term dream. Victoria needed money to buy a guitar, and Caroline worried about saving enough of her allowance, so she could buy her flute.

Only Spender had a different dream. He wanted to meet Laura again, talk to her, and get to know her better. He did not depend on money to make his dream come true; it was much more complicated.

While the teacher wrote on the board, the students took, realizing that financial independence is a multi-level feature:

Level 1: When we have money to pay for our monthly expenses and can spare a little for our dreams, we can say we have some financial independence.

Level 2: When we have money to pay for monthly expenses, spare for dreams and there is still some left in order to build up a strategic reserve for long-term savings, we can say we have good financial independence.

Level 3: When we have money to pay for monthly expenses, achieve our dreams, and our strategic reserve for long-term savings is consolidated, we can say we have excellent financial independence.

Level 4: We can reach it only in adult life when we quit working and can rest knowing that we have enough money saved for years and years to come. That is what we call financial independence.

After a while, Mr. Raymoney began to explain the subject to gauge how much the class had grasped what he had written on the board.

"Students, did you understand everything?" Mr. Raymoney asked. "This is the time to ask your questions."

"Well, I understood it, but I want to know how it's possible to be financially independent if I am living only on my allowance?" Caroline asked.

"I can understand your anxiety and your desire for financial independence," began Mr. Raymoney. "However, I assure you it is possible for anyone to reach Levels 2 and 3. It doesn't matter where your money comes from. What matters is that the money that comes into your hands is managed well."

"Even if it is a small amount?" questioned Mary.

"Yes, any amount can be enough to be saved. Of course, you have to be a little patient, too. Being patient is being smart. You can't create a strategic reserve, expecting to consolidate it within three months," said the teacher.

"The reserve you start to build now is for you to use when you turn 18. For example, to buy a car, take a longer study trip abroad, or for anything you wish for in the future."

"But what's the secret for managing our money well?" asked Victoria.

"Well, let's turn back to the four steps of the **DSOP Methodology** that I have been teaching you in the past years. If your money isn't enough, I think it's time to take back your expense notes, in order to make a diagnosis of your financial health," advised Mr. Raymoney.

The students seemed impatient in class. Money was a subject that seemed to attract everyone's attention. At their age, they naturally wished for more independence in every sense, including financial independence.

After much discussion, the bell rang to announce a break. Outside, the subject would certainly be Mr. Raymoney's class for quite a while.

Later in the week, Money Boy studied his savings and expenses. He had written some entries in his notebook that were unnecessary expenses, such as buying ice cream, chocolate, and other treats that were neither vital nor healthy.

The boy knew he should change some habits, but acknowledged that it was hard to resist some temptations. He realized he had to be strong-willed and his mind would have to be sharp.

As he was thinking, the doorbell rang and the mail carrier delivered a letter from his grandfather.

The boy was curious to read that letter, so he decided to collect his things and ran to his room. Holding the letter in his hands, he began to read.

Dear Grandson,

I read your letter with great happiness! I'm writing a list of places you must visit when you come to visit. Your granny is also very happy with your forthcoming trip and has told all her friends about it already!

Changing subjects, I am curious to know, what is DSOP? Is it any sort of a bank that lends money to people? Please don't you get yourself in trouble because of me!

As for your parents, I can talk to them and send you some money to help with the airfare. I don't have much, but I can contribute.

Please send us a picture of you in your next letter!

A hug from Grandpa!

Money Boy had a huge smile on his face when he finished reading the letter. He felt an urge to write a return letter and enclose a nice picture of himself.

He took paper and pen and started writing.

Dear Grandpa,

The DSOP Methodology is not a bank nor does it lend out money. It is just a method that helps us to make our dreams come true.

There are four steps to follow to save money and to achieve the things we wish for.

The four letters stand for Diagnosing, Dreaming, Budgeting and Saving. Whenever I put them into practice, my dreams come true.

From now on, you will receive four more letters in which I will be teaching you the pillars of that Methodology, which has helped change the lives of many people.

A big hug,
Money Boy

PS: Tell Granny I send a big kiss!

The boy sealed the envelope and headed to the post office. He wanted to leave his grandfather curious. He split the teachings of the **DSOP Methodology** into four steps, and planned to send an explanation of each one every fifteen days. The idea was for every letter to address one step of the Methodology. DSOP would be the four subjects of the letters that would teach Grandpa Raymond the meaning of Diagnosing, Dreaming, Budgeting and Saving.

While Money Boy was busy writing letters to his grandfather and taking care of his own financial life, Spender was more interested in studying at The Tune Den.

Spender convinced his father to enroll him in the music school by telling him he had always wanted to play an instrument. He even recalled that he had an electronic drum when he was a little kid, which he was passionate about playing.

Spender started attending the music school with Caroline and Victoria, which freed Money Boy from escorting the girls to Harmony.

While the two girls were striving to achieve a medium-term dream of purchasing their instruments, and Money Boy was saving to buy his plane tickets, Spender had another kind of dream in mind—winning over his first girlfriend.

He would wake up and go to sleep thinking about sweet Laura. When they met at the music school, they always smiled and waved to each other. He could not use money to buy his dream. The friendship with that girl was priceless.

Spender would have to gain her attention with gestures and attitudes that would make her happy and interested in getting to know him better. The boy didn't have much experience on the subject of dating, but he would ask Caroline for advice whenever he had the chance.

The girl would give him some tips but not very willingly. Spender, who appeared absentminded, never noticed that Caroline was very jealous of the feelings he had over the discrete and mysterious Laura.

Money Boy also noticed the way Caroline behaved near Spender. To him, her jealousy was a sign that the feelings she had about Spender were more than a mere friendship.

Nevertheless, there was nothing he could do about it except mind his own business. Deep inside his heart though, he hoped the two of them to be happy.

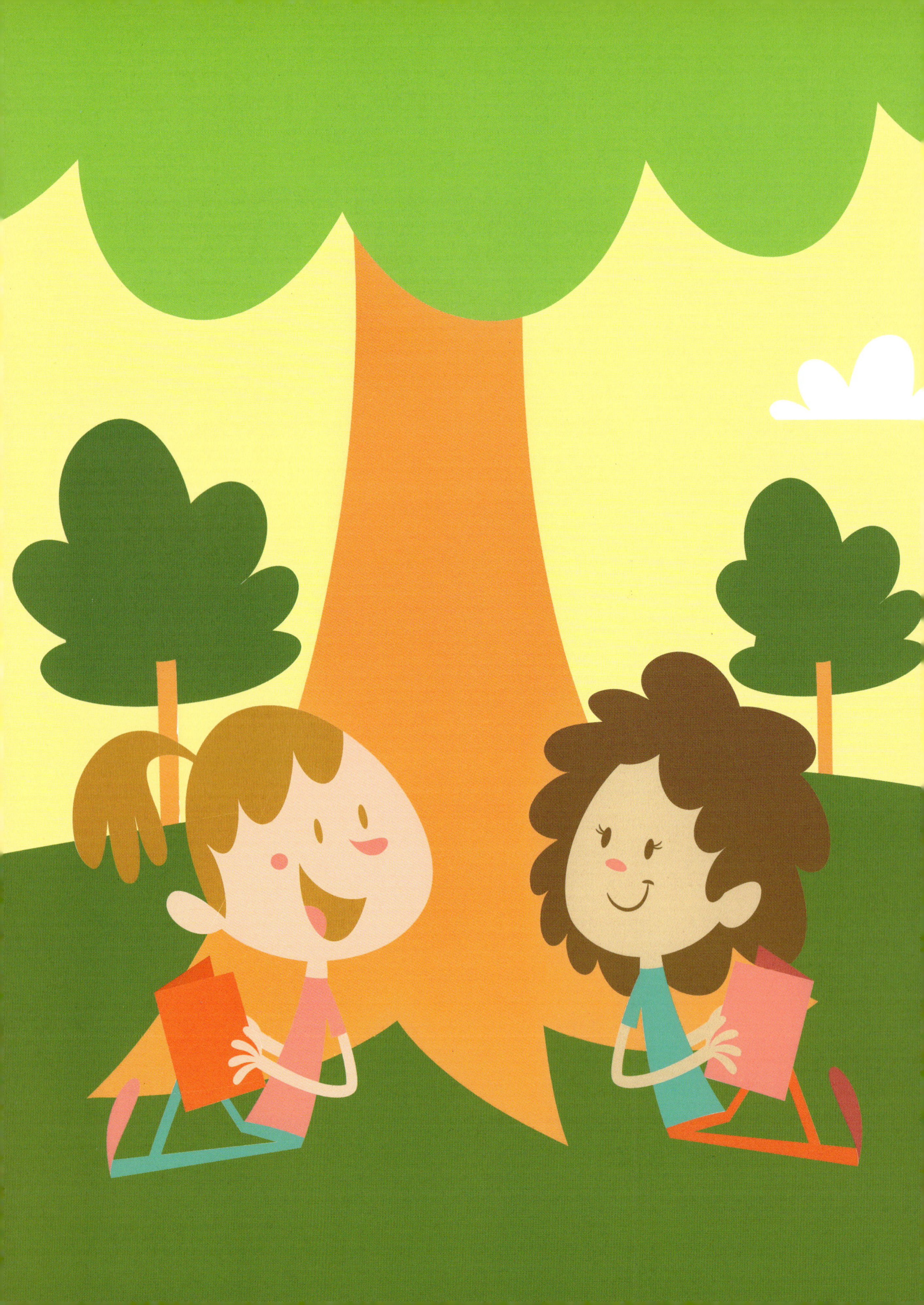

A few extra bucks

On a nice sunny afternoon, Victoria and Caroline happily talked under a mulberry tree in Daisy´s Square. Each one held a diary but not an ordinary one.

The two friends made up a financial diary where they would write down the dreams they wished to achieve. They listed how much each dream cost, how much they intended to save per month for it, and how long it would take to come true.

The girls realized they needed more money to buy the musical instruments they were learning how to play at music school.

They could not rehearse at home, and they needed to have their own instruments. In the middle of the conversation, Caroline had an idea.

"Victoria, have you thought about us making something to sell to people?" she asked.

"How's that? Making what for example?" questioned the girl, without realizing what her friend was up to.

"Well, I don't know but I think I just had an idea. Do you remember when I wrote a book last year, as the arts assignment?" Caroline recalled.

"Yes, I do."

"What if I thought about other funny stories about a group of friends at school, taking trips together," Caroline started to say.

"Go on," said Victoria.

"Well, I could come up with other stories, and we could sell booklets to people at school and also at the music school," explained Caroline. "You write beautifully, everyone can read your calligraphy, so I thought maybe you could help me put those stories on paper."

"That's a cool idea! I already loved it!" Victoria cried out with excitement. "I can grab a bunch of paper at home and we can set up each booklet together. My father works in a factory that wastes lots of paper and he brings it home. I've already seen my mother making diaries, notebooks, agendas, and stuff like that. I can make it too. It might not become as good as hers, but we can try."

"Wow, that's awesome!" said Caroline. "Let's join our talents and we can make some extra money to add to our allowance. That way we can purchase both the flute and the guitar we want a little faster."

"Yes, but we can't say anything to our parents or teachers, because they keep saying we're too young to work," warned Victoria.

"That's fine with me. Nobody needs to know. The important thing is that we make a little extra money," Caroline smiled in agreement.

The two friends left the square and walked to Victoria's house to test their idea using paper, color pens, and glue.

While Victoria assembled some booklet models, Caroline jotted down a new story. Both of them excited with the plan they had come up and happy to be working with something they liked doing.

Victoria loved handicraft work and had a talent for making things. As for Caroline, inventing stories felt like traveling to the stars and coming back to Earth.

Meanwhile, Money Boy wrote another letter to Grandpa Raymond.

Dear Grandpa,

This is the first of the four letters I promised to write to tell you about the DSOP Methodology.

Step 1, as I told you before, is Diagnosing. You can run a diagnosis of your money and find out your financial health.

To do it, take note of your expenses every day in the small expense notebook, which I am sending to you along with this letter. Keep doing that for thirty days.

I bet you must be thinking, why should I diagnose my expenses? Well, that's important because after the thirty days you'll be able to analyze your notes, and you'll see you are spending money on things that maybe aren't that important.

My teacher Mr. Raymoney taught me to do this. He explained that when we look closely at where our money is going, we start to choose more carefully on what we buy. We use our common sense and become aware that some things are more important than others. Those that are not necessary can be cut out of our day-to-day purchases.

The first step is for you to make an honest evaluation of your financial life!

In the next letter, I'll explain to you about the second step of the DSOP Methodology: Dreaming.

A big hug,
Money Boy

THE TUNE DEN

So near, so faraway

A few weeks later, while walking in the hallway of The Tune Den, Spender panicked and almost fainted. Victoria and Caroline came to help, as he was white as a sheet and his forehead sweaty as if he had a fever.

His face looked sad and he walked slowly.

Victoria and Caroline didn't understand anything. Spender asked them to take him out of there and they went outside. After he caught his breath, he thanked his friends and noticed Caroline holding his hand very hard.

Her hand was warm and a little sweaty from being nervous. Caroline had become so worried, that Spender suddenly realized she really cared about him.

"Spender, what happened? Are you feeling ok?" Victoria asked.

"Yes, I think so. I saw something that made me very sad," he answered.

"What did you see?" asked Caroline, holding his hand firmly.

"I saw Laura kissing another guy in the school hall. I think he is her boyfriend, because they were walking, holding hands, just like a couple," Spender replied.

At that point, Caroline let go of his hand and began to complain.

"Oh, so that's it! What a foolish thing! There's nothing special about that girl," Caroline lashed out. "I don't know why you're so crazy about her. She's skinny, she has one eye bigger than the other, and I don't know if you guys have noticed, but she dresses really bad. Why on earth would someone wear plaid pants with a striped blouse and flowered sneakers? It is in such bad taste."

Spender and Victoria stared at their friend with their mouths open. They didn't know what to say after so much criticism coming from Caroline about Laura. The three remained silent and eventually went to their classrooms.

The following day, Victoria mentioned to her friend that she overreacted the day before. Caroline agreed and promised she would never get in the middle of all that romantic confusion again with such an annoying boy as Spender.

During break time, Money Boy offered a supportive shoulder to Spender, who had been teary-eyed after he found out Laura already had a boyfriend.

"Dude, aren't you looking for a girlfriend in the wrong place? I think that Laura is not the right girl for you. Look around, there must be other girls, more interesting, friendlier, and funnier," advised Money Boy.

"Ah, I don't know! I've never looked at girls that way. When I became more independent and started riding buses, making decisions, and managing my money with the help of Mr. Raymoney's classes, well, all of that made me change and wish for new things," Spender explained.

"I know how it feels. We are growing up!" Money Boy said.

"I want to have the independence to date girls! But before that, I've got to find a girl who wants the same thing, and one who likes me, too. And, she needs to be cool, funny, and pretty," summed up Spender.

"But tell me something, of all the girls you have met in your life, which one is the coolest, funniest, and prettiest?" Money Boy asked.

"Well, let me think. Ah, there's Giselle, but she's not that pretty. Hmmm, there's Anna Claire, but she's not very funny," replied Spender, searching for an answer.

"Isn't there anyone left?" asked Money Boy.

"Ahh, there's Claudia. Hmm, not Claudia, no. Her parents won't let her out of the house to do anything alone. She's a girl with no independence at all," explained Spender.

"And who's the girl you know that has independence, is funny, pretty, and cool?" asked Money Boy one more time.

"Wow, Caroline's face popped up in my head right now. That's weird!" said Spender, surprised and smiling.

"Weird? How come?" asked the boy.

"Ah, I don't know exactly. Because she is our friend, because she's a little crazy, and because..." Spender stopped what he was saying.

"Look, I think Caroline is all that you said and there's something else that's very important," the boy said.

"What else?" Spender asked.

"She loves you! She really cares about you. Everybody sees that except you," Money Boy revealed to his friend.

"Wow, now I am confused! Caroline would make a nice girlfriend. Why hadn't I thought about that before? She has always been so close and yet so far away," concluded Spender.

The two guys walked to the computer classroom where another class with Mrs. Sunday was about to begin.

Spender couldn't stop thinking about Caroline. In his head, he listed her qualities and imperfections, and it was undeniable that the qualities exceeded the imperfections.

The girl was pretty, funny, and had achieved her independence in the beginning of the semester after communicating with her parents. She could take buses alone in town and had enrolled in music school. She was about to buy her flute with the money she earned from the sales of the booklets she made with Victoria.

While Spender thought about all that, he watched his friend sitting by his side. Money Boy was writing another letter to his grandfather on a single sheet of paper that glided over the table.

After each line, Money Boy would pause and wonder about what he was writing. After much discussion about all the comings and goings of his friend Spender's love life, he scratched his head and wondered.

Should I find a girl to date, too? Can I expect the game of love to give me more independence, allowing me to grow up faster? Well, if there was a girl that could be my ideal match, she would be Victoria for sure. Ever since I met her, I have never found another girl as special and as funny as her. Besides, she is Money Girl. Apparently, she is my perfect match, but is she thinking about dating or is it too early for us to talk about it?

The thoughts were brewing in his mind. The image of Victoria's smiling face would come up whenever he closed his eyes. He tried hard to focus on writing a letter to his grandfather, so he picked up the pen on the table and began to write.

Dear Grandpa,

In this letter, I'm going to introduce you to Step 2 of the DSOP Methodology, which is Dreaming.

We should always have in mind three kinds of dreams that we want to come true. The first one is the short-term dream (due to come true within one month); the second one is the medium-term dream (due to come true within three months); and, lastly, the long-term dream (due to come true within six months).

In order to estimate the time to achieve each dream, you must write on a sheet of paper two important questions:

How much is each dream worth?

How much am I saving each month for each dream?

For example, my current dream is to purchase the airline tickets to take my trip.

Dream: airline tickets

Cost: $650

Savings per month: $80

Therefore, my dream will take approximately eight months to come true, if I manage to save $80 per month and if the airline ticket fares do not increase.

As you can see, it is a medium to long-term dream, and I am working really hard to achieve it.

Well, I've got to go now.

I'll write you more next time.

A big hug,
Money Boy

THE TUNE DEN

The month of June

The end of the semester was near. Caroline and Victoria had managed to sell their story booklets to a few friends at school and to some students at the music school.

Their friends were impressed with the stories and with the artistic bookbinding.

Besides having fun creating the booklets, the two friends also managed to save a good amount of money for their long-term dreams.

With that money, Caroline and Victoria went over to a music store, bargained and got 10% off their purchase, because they paid cash.

They returned home very happy carrying a flute and a guitar. However, their mothers wanted to know where they got the money to buy the instruments.

Both girls found an easy way to explain about making and selling the booklets. The mothers were not very happy, but were proud of what their daughters had achieved anyway.

Victoria and Caroline showed determination, hard work, and courage to achieve their dreams. They applied the **DSOP Methodology** for five long months and always saved some money from their allowance to make the purchase of the musical instruments possible. With discipline and intelligence, they had achieved their goals.

Money Boy's dream was close to becoming reality as well. He talked with his parents and proved he was mature and responsible enough to take a trip by himself. He explained to his mother everything he had learned from Mr. Raymoney about independence and asked her to trust him.

The boy's parents said they needed a couple of days before making their decision. They knew they should gradually give their son a certain amount of independence, but they were afraid that the trip to Brazil was too big a step to take.

However, the boy's grandfather influenced the decision making of Mrs. Foresight and Mr. Unaware. Grandpa Raymond said he missed his grandson very much and promised to take care of him. He softened their hearts by saying, "No one could ever refuse such a request from an old man."

The parents gave Money Boy their permission to travel and the boy was very happy. Two weeks later, a letter from the grandfather arrived with three $100 bills and a $50 bill, to help the boy purchase the airline tickets.

Money Boy rushed to the bank and deposited the money in his savings account where he had been saving all his money. After that, he went back home to write another letter to his grandpa.

Dear Grandpa,

Here I am once again! This time I'm writing about Step 3 of the DSOP Methodology, which is Budgeting.

Have you ever noticed that most people spend all their money throughout the month and don't save anything?

In the DSOP Methodology, budgeting means taking part of the money we earn each month and saving it in a piggy bank or a savings account.

After doing that, we can use the rest of the money to pay for our monthly expenses.

Our mistake is earning our salary or allowance and using it to pay our bills. Afterwards, if there's something left, we save a small amount.

The thing is that way there's never going to be any money left, don't you think?

In the DSOP Budget, first we save the money for the dream and then we use what's left to pay regular monthly expenses.

Well, I was very happy after I got your letter with the $350. I've already deposited that money in the bank and there is only a small amount missing for my dream to come true.

Everything is going to be all right! During vacation, in July, I'll be there!

A big hug,
Money Boy

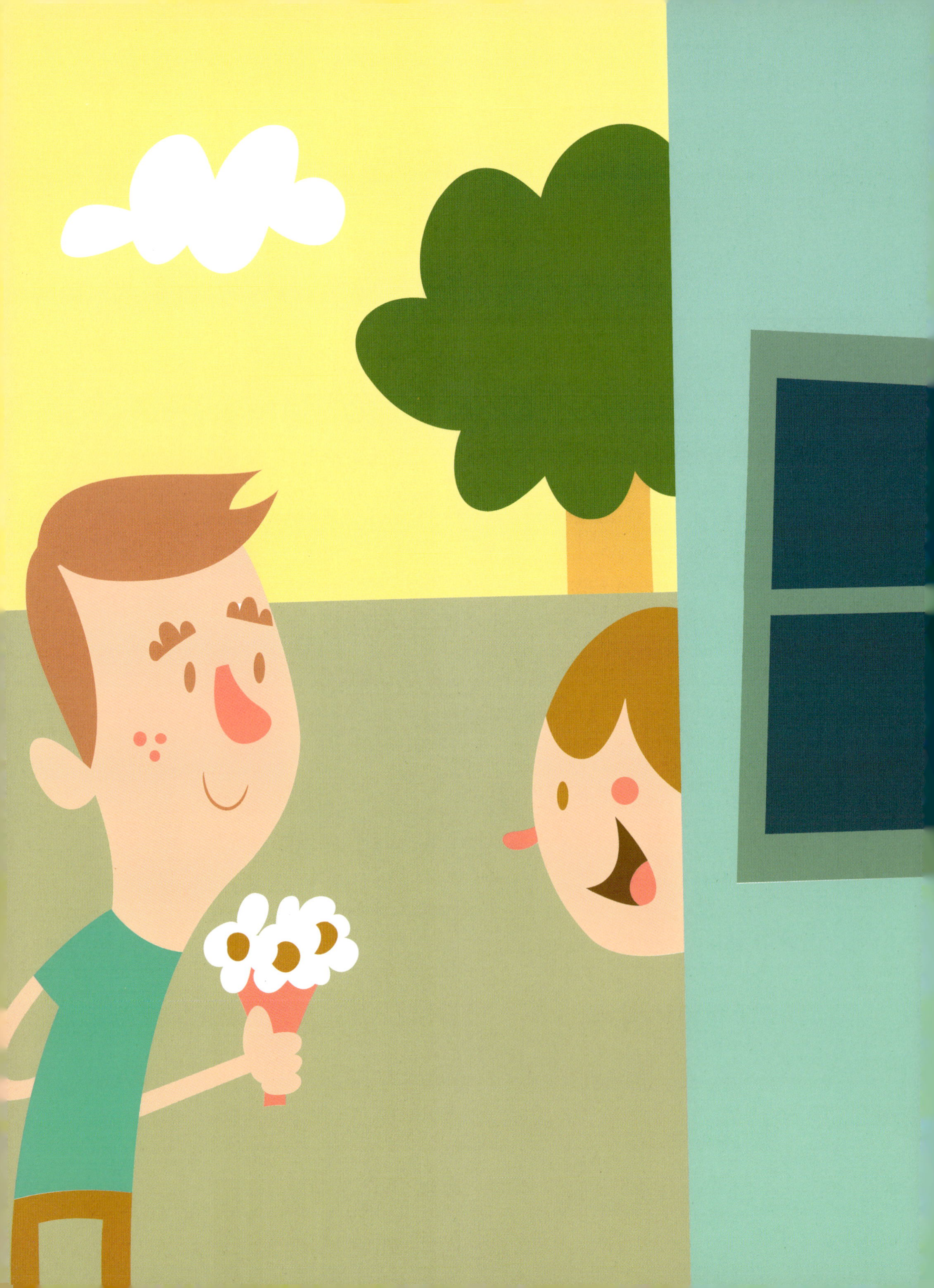

Flowers to you!

The final exam week had arrived. At school, the students were getting ready for vacation. They still had to turn in their final assignments and were committed to getting good grades.

In the middle of all that, Spender was the only one in Money Boy's group of friends who hadn't realized his dream yet. Spender knew that the ideal girlfriend had always been by his side, but he didn't have a clue as to how to win her over.

Confused and lost, he decided to ask his father for help. The boy told him he wanted to have a "man's talk."

After Spender explained his situation, his father suggested he should invest in simple gestures, like inviting Caroline to the movies, holding her hand, and giving her flowers.

The boy treasured his father's advice and thanked him. Some days later, Spender knocked on Caroline's door holding a flower bouquet. She opened the door and he said, "I got you these flowers!"

The girl had a big smile and words just didn't come out of her mouth.

She didn't know exactly what to say and simply thanked him. Spender invited her over to the movies the following Saturday and she said yes.

The boy left full of hope and Caroline ran to her room enjoying the scent of the flowers she had received.

Saturday came and both went to watch a movie called Summer's Dream. Eventually, they held hands sitting in the dark theater. On their way out, Spender asked Caroline if she wanted to be his girlfriend.

After a minute of suspense, she said she would love to. They walked together holding hands.

Meanwhile, at Victoria's house, Money Boy had been helping her study for the final math exam. In a break between lessons, they mentioned that maybe Spender had already made his girlfriend's dream come true.

Both laughed and Money Boy decided to ask the girl with the dimples a question:

"Victoria, do you ever think about dating someone?"

"Yes I do. It's just that I don't know if anyone is going to like me the way Spender seems to like Caroline," she replied.

"You are a very special girl. It's impossible not to like a girl like you!" Money Boy said.

"Ah, you are embarrassing me!" Victoria said.

"You know, ever since you showed up at school, on that rainy day, distracted and dropping your stuff on the ground, I wanted to become friends with you. When I helped you stand up and saw the little dimples on your face, I realized there was a very special girl right there," Money Boy confided.

"What do you mean by all that?" asked Victoria.

"Ah, I don't know! Ever since Spender mentioned this love independence thing, I began thinking about it," he said.

"What? Love independence?" asked Victoria, laughing!

"Sounds funny, doesn't it? We've learned at Mr. Raymoney's class about three kinds of independence: individual, citizen, and financial. But our friend Spender made up another one—love independence." said the boy, laughing.

"Are you trying to be independently in love?" Victoria asked with a smile.

"I was thinking about who I´d like to have as my first girlfriend. I thought hard and I wouldn't like to date anyone now except you!" Money Boy said in a soft voice.

"Wow! I don't know what to say," answered Victoria.

"Well, I know I'll be traveling soon. I'm spending thirty days away. But if you could wait for me, I promise I'll be the best boyfriend any girl could have when I'm back here," Money Boy assured her.

Victoria gave a broad smile. Her eyes were shining as she nodded in agreement. Victoria had always been his best friend, keeping him company, and she was the sweetest girl in the world. Money Boy felt his heart beating faster.

Victoria was the first person to whom Money Boy had taught the **DSOP Methodology** a couple of years ago. She learned quickly and turned into a smart girl who pursued her dreams and would pass the financial lessons on to anyone who was interested.

He was very proud of her and had always felt that if he ever was to date someone, that someone would be her. That afternoon, they made a love commitment to each other and Victoria promised she would wait for Money Boy to come back from his trip.

As soon as he arrived home, the boy wrote another letter to his grandfather. He wanted to tell him the news and to reveal the last step in the **DSOP Methodology**.

He had so many things to say he filled up two whole pages. When he finished, he put them into an envelope and enclosed a picture of Victoria.

Dear Grandpa,

Today something amazing happened! I began dating the most special and smartest girl at school. Her name is Victoria. We've been friends for a long time and I've always liked her.

Now I think I'm becoming an adult because I have financial, citizen, individual and love independence. Laughing here!

Well, we are almost there with the teaching of the DSOP Methodology, and I'll be arriving in Brazil soon as well!

So let's move on.

Step 4 in the DSOP Methodology is Saving. Saving means keeping your money.

The more money we save, the quicker we make our dreams come true!

When I was a boy, I used to keep my money in a piggy bank. I didn't know it at that time, but I was already practicing the act of saving money. My mother taught me that.

Currently, I have a savings account that my parents helped me open.

Whenever I deposit money in it, I make more money with interest rates.

It's a funny thing. Whenever I put money in my account, the bank also puts in a little money to help me.

Mr. Raymoney told me there are some investments that can give me more money than my savings account. He promised to tell me about them next semester, so I'll be able to invest in them, too.

If you find it interesting, go talk to your bank manager and maybe he can tell you about those investments as well.

After we begin saving money, it feels like addiction. We can't stop saving.

Well, my nickname says it all, right?

Love,
Money Boy

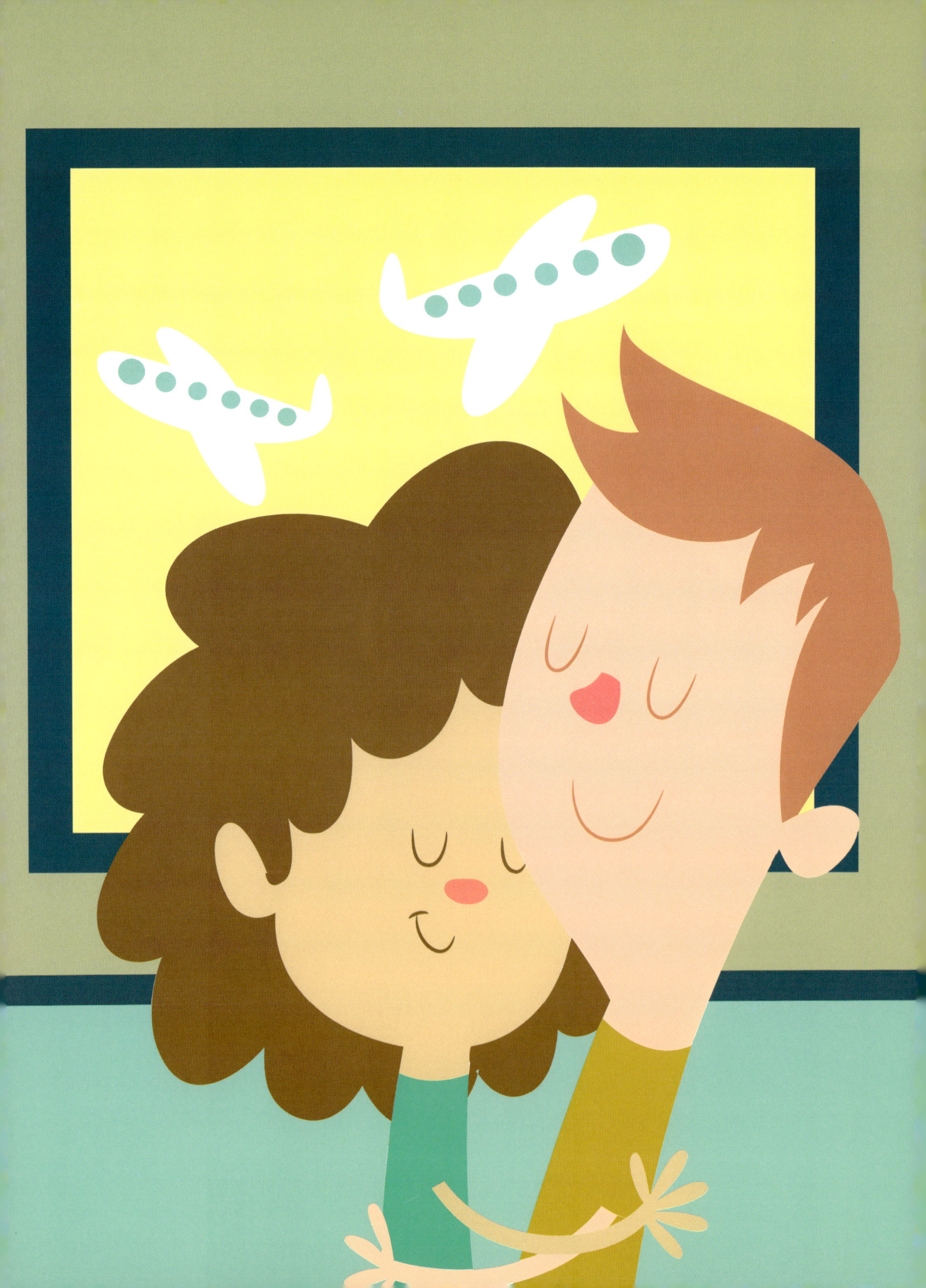

Ready to takeoff

July had finally come. Victoria and Caroline would use their free time to work even harder on their music lessons.

Spender had decided to drop the music school and practice judo, which had always been his passion.

As for Money Boy, he was packing up with the help of his mother to depart within a few hours. His destiny was the town where his grandparents lived and they were very anxious waiting for him.

Half of his heart wanted very much to travel, but the other half wanted to stay and was sad because he would spend thirty days away from sweet Victoria.

"Son, time will fly! You will have so much fun and will be back here without even noticing," said Mrs. Foresight.

"Mom, Victoria said she is going to wait for me, but what if she meets some other guy that makes her forget about me?" Money Boy said concerned.

"She is not going to do that, believe me. Every love story has a difficult period along the way," said his mother.

"How's that? What difficult period?" the boy asked.

"It's a period to test your love. Just like a school exam to test if it's real," explained the mother.

"It's easier to understand if I think of it that way," answered the boy.

"So do it! Pay attention to your wise mother's advice, because I've outlived you both," remarked Mrs. Foresight with a smile.

"That's true mom! You are always giving me good advice. I remember when I was a kid and you gave me my first piggy bank. So much has happened since then. As Mr. Raymoney has taught us, you are younger longer than me. And, I am younger less time than you!" said the boy.

"That's true, son. I've taught you to save coins to make dreams come true and now you're right here, a grownup, packing up your bag to take a trip alone. Enjoy your stay with your grandparents, but come back soon because we'll miss you very much, and so will Victoria," ended Mrs. Foresight with tears in her eyes.

A few hours later, Money Boy was about to enter the boarding room when he heard someone calling his name.

He looked back and saw Victoria. She ran to him and gave him a big hug. Then she opened up a small box she held in her hands and removed a neck chain. She hung it around his neck and gave him a kiss, explaining that the chain was a piece of her that would forever be close to him.

After saying goodbye, Money Boy boarded the plane and took his seat.

The captain announced, "Ladies and gentlemen, cabin crew, we are ready for takeoff!"

He buckled up, held tight the chain Victoria had given him and looked out at the sky. He told himself he had a blessed life!

Author
Reinaldo Domingos

www.reinaldodomingos.com.br

Reinaldo Domingos is a master degree, professor, educator, and financial therapist. Author of the books: Financial Therapy; Allowance is not just about money; Get rid of debts; I deserve to have money; Money Boy—family dreams; Money Boy—goes to school; Money Boy—friends helping friends; Money Boy—in a sustainable world; Money Boy—little citizen; Money Boy—time for changes; The Boy and the Money; The Boy, the Money, and the Three Piggy Banks; The Boy, the Money, and the Anthopper; Being wealthy is not a secret; and the series Wealth is not a secret.

In 2009 he created Brazil's first textbook series of financial education aimed at grammar school, already in use by several schools in the country, both private and public. In 2012 he was a pioneer in creating the first financial education program for young apprentices. In 2013 that program also included young adults. In 2014 he created the first financial education course for entrepreneurs, followed by financial education as a university extension course.

Domingos graduated in Accounting and System Analysis. He is the founder of Confirp Accounting and Consulting and was the governor of Rotary International District 4610 (2009-2010). Currently, he is the CEO of DSOP Financial Education and DSOP Publishing. He is the mentor, founder and president of Abef (Brazilian Association of Financial Educators). He is also the creator of Brazil's first postgraduate course in Financial Education and Coaching and mentor of the **DSOP Methodology**.